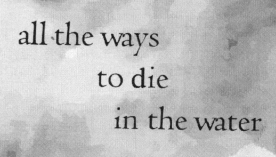

all·the ways to die in the water

Nik Xandir Wolf

all the ways

to die

in the water

by

Nik Xandir Wolf

Kelp Books, LLC

ISBN-13: 978-1-7373228-5-6

Cover design by: Katarina Naskovski
Library of Congress Control Number: 2022941502
Printed in the United States of America

for my mom

part 1 – land

wanderlust

does the small world feel so small
when our hearts still get lost in the music
of small clubs, in the rhythm of the open road,
in blues notes, like a drifter's melody?
eyes closed tight, the scent of sweat and cologne
and coco mademoiselle
and stale beer
and hot whisky
when jazz dancing feet shuffle, interlace
scuffing dusty floors where the
flecked surface glitters in a curtain
of filtered moonlight
the jingle of foreign currency
in the zipper pocket of a weathered backpack
a drum beat down arteries
city corridors
marble cities
an echo so close
it can't be held
finger-tips over greying
edges of timeless statues
gilded and stoic. obsession.
the wayfarers, the insects,
the lapping of waves against
ankles and toes
two lovers

maybe three
drifting over a tropical shore.
lost again.
again.

ants

small black ants
against the smooth surface
they appear to curry favor
with a small force
living inside the drain
in my guest bathroom.
there is a lifeforce down there
and they appear to have an arrangement.
their tiny wagons are circling.
i try to wash them down
but they march back up the drain, fortified.
somehow.
by the gods of sterling throats
they arrive again resilient
the little search party
of intrepid wanderers.
It's a mutiny.
they know they can defeat me.
easily. they march up corroded
pipes toward the shimmering
floodless porcelain.
it is late
or early
in my pajamas
i wash my hands. invisible
particles flush away, clear as sight
and it is then that i see them
marching still. leaning
into the current. the relentless flow.

physics playing it's tricks of proportion
these creatures with their preternatural strength
mighty. tiny. soldiers.
when i dry my hands
i am inspired.
i want to be, somehow, as bold
as my tiny uninvited friends.

standing in a café at noon

the steam wand's hiss is silenced
as it dips into the canister of milk.
bubbles collide above the
the barista's work smile.
i want to capture the stillness.
the suspended universe inside
the square, fractured room.
i stand at the register
wondering if my transparent desire
is as cliché as it feels.
the want. to stir the faded irises.
blue. into my iced coffee with
half and half, and simple syrup.
and drink it all down through
the checkered paper straw.
to exist in this space, and displace
a declining cubic square measurement
of air and molecules. i watch
the digital currency get extracted
through the plastic husk
of my device. i accept the cup
of caffeine, the cheapest drug
that i haven't banned myself
from yet. and if this is a room
and i am within its confines.
this tapestry.
then our bodies

and movements
affect the calculus of this fabric.
i leave that silent thread uninhabited,
and allow the next passenger
to weave through it all, up to the register.
it feels similar, but then again it's not.
maybe i can, someday, turn it all off.
the sun and our eyes—the light.
and we could really see
what we are.
naked of our bodies.
just the anomalies we are, in the gridded
patterns of the great video game
programmer's minimized
left window. 1's and 0's
an update in progress.
like an ellipsis dotting the
spatial framework in the next line.
loading…
green interlaced signals shape my
paper cup of espresso in grids.
then, a splash against the porcelain floor.
a tall latte triple shot, swirls black on the counter top.
a cold brew thinly poured over fat cubes of ice.
the barrista disappears behind
folding doors and they swing.
until they stop.

tommy lee's not dead yet

i use a finger worn fabric
to dust the jackets of my
vinyl records and it all reminds me of cd's
there was a decade i recall in the nineties.
sometimes, high on meth
my mind would skip like the hollow
voices inside my walmart boom box.
i never play them anymore
artists like soundgarden
who can never play again— the cranberry's
will never play. michael jackson.
this ephemeral march toward
hotel room bath tubs
and oxy-methadone-suicide
is it because we stopped
worshiping them long enough?
are they like small gods
that disappear from our crowded memories.
like zeus, or odin, or aphrodite.
or is it just because
there is no room for them
in this new culture
where sound
breaks
clean and energetic
something else.
something like an
empty, buzzing electronic sound-bank.
with ai dj's

contrails

i wake with that ragged, empty feeling that
a deep rest sometimes imprints
i was dead
and will be again soon.
and everything i have ever done
never mattered anyway. and never will.
that clarity
i wonder if i'll even find pleasure in anything again
achievement
life
love
fucking
maybe the meth-lsd-cocaine-weed-malt liquor-meth-
oxy-alcohol-xanax-adderall. has sucked me dry of my
sweet serotonin
little powder-blue vampires
leeching at the dregs of my spirit.
i was born with regulatory issues
i needed to understand the why's
and how's and all i get are vague
clues hidden somewhere between
pleasure and pain
i need relief from unbearable urges,
even if i don't *really* exist.
the sky, it is always grey
today a shallow gray
like the tule fog of my childhood
where i could sneak back into the furnace
heated covers of my small bed. the last
place, that i can recall, where i felt the promise of life.
the central valley and it's undulating hills

the horizon of jagged mountains
i can see both heaven and hell then
and now it's the loop that I'm stuck in
it is hell. it is hate. it is bombs
and waking up from a deep sleep
wishing i were dead like
the frozen irrigation ditch
behind that farm
where i drank-in sub-freezing temperatures.
waiting for the school bus
a burning funicular cloud of diesel fumes.
the square, breath fogged window
watching a crack form in the clouds
two ventricular veins
pulsate like the arteries of a pagan god.
a pair of contrails bleeding slowly into cold blue

table

i can feel real grains on the surface of the wooden table.
but i have been fooled before.
sometimes the industrial composites are more real.
somehow.
i can draw my finger along the border
and find the edge of its surface. i can wrap my hands
around
its edges. it is finite, and i like that about it.
i crave that about it
i like that i know where it begins, and where it ends.
i like to think that i too, am finite.
that i can narrate myself a beginning, middle and end.
i can do as i wish with this body. this space.
it has a beginning, middle and end. i can wrap
myself into a ball so tightly and squeeze
until i disappear in a bright, yellow burst.
a swirl of carbon dust
i can redesign myself
come back and stand
with my brand new, state-of-the-art genes.
with all of the top-tier modifications
even red eyes and royal blue knuckles.

love fern

a once dead fern is calibrated against a rusted fence
outside my window. i thought it was dead
it was dead. then, overnight
it grew two long, dark tendrils that reached
skyward like octopus arms writhing and twisting
and gripping for things.
when i dream about you and the way you
you twisted around me
while we slept together all those years
when you talked in your sleep
something about feral celebrities
and domesticated rodents
when i reached out to touch you
before you left.
you wilted, too
the fern is gone
the hill was scraped away
by a gardeners shovel
and you are metal like that, too
more like shrapnel, though.
lodged somewhere where i will never quite heal.

getting ghosted

he's sitting there at the same table checking his phone
with a vulnerability that is usually reserved for
first dates. it can be assumed that they met online
because he clearly has no idea if the digital self is
similar to the actual self, much like this person's own
profile
that shows him ten years younger and with a full head of
hair.
maybe he feels like he's getting ghosted. maybe
he's waiting for his tinder date to materialize
like internet pixels forming into the shape of his dreams.
maybe it will be like that 80's movie where the nerds
get the model to come to life, *weird science.*
only now it kind of does work like that. well, it's supposed
to.
but what am i waiting for in front of sweating glass of iced
coffee?
it's possible that this is all a dream,
and the ghosts i call to are images conjured
by dreams and the whole space is imaginary.
is a dream real if you can't feel the world your touch?
do you stake a flag in the drifting sand
and let the somnolent images sift through your fingers
like sand shaped pictures, slowly
falling
down
emptying the vessel.

the high watermarks of time.
is the sound i hear just
god's long robes flapping against her
rigid arms
arms that reach for me,
and always miss.

part 2 - water

disembarkation

there was a sign on the old ship that pointed
the way in little faded arrows toward disembarkation.
a space for exiting passengers to stage-left in an
emergency.
the ship swayed on ripples in the current too small and too
infinite.
and it made me wonder why i consider the ocean lonely?
it's possible that it prefers its inverse world of slow
solitude.
her plume of ragged hair matriculating around her
shoulders
as if in some trick of the light, of slowed stop-time
animation.
and who am i? some morally superior annex, shouldering
the weight of whispering sun and inexorable gravity.
traversing these great swaths of land and attempting to right
my permanently withering posture.
we think we are old and or worthy.
but nothing is old as nothing exists
even if we did once exist
we don't now
we flicker out like the tender filament of a light bulb.
something will replace us. the world needs more.
god needs more
god in her big shimmering silent wilderness.
she shrugs
and we ride further on her rippling surface
on this ship.

frankenfish

reanimated. a fish and some sort of toad
creature get spliced up
and recombined
a new strand of dna replicates
and wham bam.
if science can do it then why the fuck not?
do it. just always do it.
at any cost.
little crspr-cas9 babies.
if we created a fish that grows
ten times faster in its pond water
landfill.
if that instant fish
the spiny dorsal fins
slithering in brackish ponds
this toad vessel. this vascular murmuring.
this beating, bleating, corpuscle. churning in liquid.
finds its natural way.
even if its not natural.
sprouts spliced legs
and slips away. away
lands
crawls
to the ocean
to the rest of our fish species.
toward the slack and swell and ruin of sea.

shark boy
in memory of todd endris

the cobalt of the pacific in the winter is brighter.
a phosphorescent blue. electrified
with phyto-plankton. it's a cold blue.
it's a color you have no eyes for. it's a color that
hides the flash of white scales and jagged
teeth that gather in furious inertia.
a guileless chafing. taps sounding on trumpets
through speakers around the presidio.
franks sinatra crooning *my way*. cranked up.
because the drifting wings of red
that emanate from the broken ridges
of your fiberglass surfboard sing too.
harmonies overlapping in sonic discordance.
three separate interactions. three separate
struggles as skin peels away from bone.
a dolphin pod arrives at the zenith
and you get away.
a spotlight drifting toward a waxing polar shore.
you won't die. not on this day.
you will never die.

reins

it started early
the thrill
of words tumbling down
the page
she reached across
and pulled them
to her
reins spun like webs
tethered to glistening
fractured pieces
of her universe
of reality
gathered tightly in her fists
she became
she became that captain
voyaging a tameless
sea

winter days

rivulets. the foamy sea streams over the tip
of my surfboard when i paddle steadily
into the stormy bay. waves come down
over my head like ice bats
that crack
in painful throbs
i struggle against the rip-tide
the panic starts to hit
that i can't do this
that i won't make it back
to see my son
the fatigue.
i reverse course and keep
rowing until my arms give out.
the sets keep coming.
waves folding in on themselves
pinning me into
a spin-dry
crashing into submerged rocks
a tennis ball served up speedy and fresh.
my feet touch sand
i push forward
upward, clawing for breath
rows of seals bobbing like
moorings loosed in a storm.
when rain and wind swept the pacific.

i wait for another wave
to crash over my past.
more always come.
so do days, even as
they shorten each year
and the nights are longer
i am not young
anymore.
they were pages
in a faded children's book.
all those waves i missed.
all the lives
that came before me that are gone.
the human collective, though
can keep crashing, starboard, like the sea.
i will stay there
inside it
where it is cold
like me

church

i had to go to church
as a child.
it seemed like an unnecessary
complication.
now i don't go
but for the weddings
i've been to this church
in monterey
exactly twice
in three years.
for a wedding,
and for a funeral. the
same man was the subject
of both ceremonies.
which
the second visitation,
when the bell clangored
in its post-adobe arch
his wife's
teary face had changed from
those happy, squinting tears
of joy
of promise
of hope
this this
at this old catholic
church and the cast iron bell
that tolls for weddings,
tolls to mark time,

and tolls for him.
this time.
and it's this old bell
that i can't stop hearing.
this ceremony,
this procession
he's gone.
we thought we knew more.
but we didn't know
these small things.
these articulate
floral displays
of hydrangea
and rose, and carnation.
hold photos
of his hunting dog.
and his two tiny children
cuddled in their crying
mothers swaddling arms.

duck blind

it is almost eight thirty now
and the sun is fully above the horizon
i'm still rooted in camo and alert
the sight on my shotgun glints
and i'm afraid it will spook the birds

four pelts of bloody feathers are in front
of my four foot by four foot cement tube
dug into an island on the columbia
owned for generations by a good friend

the river rushes around the
shore and the i'm afraid a small wave
will carry my ducks away. one more
is all i need and i'll row back home.

a shot rings off to the south and i see a
fat male mallard get peppered, but flies
and he's coming right at me, the beautiful
green velvet of his neck and i train my
shotgun and pull the trigger.

the splash is just beyond my canoe
and my dog is tired from fighting the
current, he's done good and i can get it. i pull

myself from the blind, straining against
the neoprene waders jammed with gear.

the dog jumps in the canoe. i wade out to
tie up the inert body, only it twitches
and he's not quite dead so i step quickly,
reach for it, so it doesn't dive on me
so i can break its neck and hang it

he dives so i reach in for him. i feel
the body, but can't quite grip him, i
wish i had put the shotgun in the boat
with the dog. i reach deeper and realize
my mistake too late. the icy waters

of the columbia pour into my waders
my nuts shoot up into my stomach. i step back
toward the island, toward the boat. but the water
rushes in. my footing gives and i realize
with a quick inhale of water and air that i have no

more footing. it's just water and current and
i am coughing. only i can't fucking swim in
this goddam gear. i know my only hope is
to remove it. i tear away at the boots, the dog
jumps to me, i can't reach the straps; i inhale

i'm tumbling through dark water, eyes closed
she's the first thing that i can think of. her
and my newborn and my toddler. i tear harder

at the strap and it cuts into my hand. i tumble deeper.
i need a goddamn breath. i tear at the waders.
i keep tearing. until the water and the current turn peaceful
and i stop.

hemingway's headstone

the grass is browning at its edges, under melting snow.
a corrugated iron gate greets me when i park.
i'm in ketchum.
i am only surprised at the utter silence. it is empty.

it seems odd to think of the legend that lies beneath
this partially frozen soil and that i am the only
person here to pay homage. the snow beneath my shoe
yields a satisfying crunch and i wonder if people are afraid
to see the deceased because it reminds them of the clock.

three large pines surround the massive head stone.
i kneel as if to speak to him. to see if i can bring
him any comfort. to see if i deserve a nod from his spirit.
i am selfish and i want him to impart his gift to me,
somehow.

i provide an offering, a bottle of california wine
and set it on his grave.
i imagine he would have liked to try it.
i set it next to the scattering of coins. a token
tossed through to the afterlife. a coin to buy a beer.
how do i take him with me? how do i make him live again?
i pull up a stone, but it isn't mine to take.
instead i scratch the earth.

the soil is sticky and clings to my knuckles. i scratch
harder, i dig, and my finger finds a root. i grip it firmly.
i feel it's depth, its age. it has grown inside and through
the body below. i pull at it, as if to keep it, but instead
it pulls me. it begins to grow, and fast. sliding up my wrist,
the sleeve of my shirt. it wends around my arm,
over my face and through my eye sockets my ears,
my mouth.
i feel it there. it pulls me down and it's cold and damp.
i look for that coin, and i find it. i place it on the nearest
juke box.
i order us another round and when the song plays,
i drink.

About Nik Xandir Wolf

Nik Xandir Wolf grew up in California's Central Valley. He moved to Monterey years ago and picked up surfing as a form of recovery. He has worked in various fields and has volunteered for many organizations. His most rewarding volunteer position was held at CASA, where he represented abused and neglected children in the juvenile dependency system in court as a Guardian Ad Litem. He spent 12 years with that organization.

Nik is an avid reader, writer, performer, and host of the Rubber Chicken Poetry Slam. He reads poetry while surfing, drinks rum with the lost boys, and sets sail when the seas get far too rough. His favorite place on earth is inside a bookstore.

Nik Xandir Wolf is published in various magazines and journals. He received his MFA from UC Riverside - Palm Desert. He also attended Stanford's OWC program in Novel Writing.

Made in the USA
Columbia, SC
08 February 2023

11377750R00020